A CHILD'S BOOK OF POEMS

PICTURES BY
GYO FUJIKAWA

GROSSET & DUNLAP · PUBLISHERS · NEW YORK
A FILMWAYS COMPANY

ISBN: 0-448-14341-0
Library of Congress Catalog Card Number: 77-73203

Contents

NIGHT

The sun descending in the west,
  The evening star does shine;
The birds are silent in their nest,
  And I must seek for mine.
The moon, like a flower,
In heaven's high bower,
With silent delight
Sits and smiles on the night.

Farewell, green fields and happy groves,
  Where flocks have took delight.
Where lambs have nibbled, silent moves
  The feet of angels bright;
Unseen they pour blessing,
And joy without ceasing,
On each bud and blossom,
And each sleeping bosom.

William Blake

WHICH IS THE WAY TO SOMEWHERE TOWN?

Which is the way to Somewhere Town?
  Oh, up in the morning early;
Over the tiles and the chimney pots,
  That is the way, quite clearly.

And which is the door to Somewhere Town?
  Oh, up in the morning early;
The round red sun is the door to go through,
  That is the way, quite clearly.

Kate Greenaway

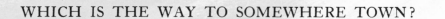

SUMMER SUN

Great is the sun, and wide he goes
Through empty heaven without repose.
And in the blue and glowing days
More thick than rain he showers his rays.

Though closer still the blinds we pull
To keep the shady parlor cool,
Yet he will find a chink or two
To slip his golden fingers through.

The dusty attic spider-clad
He, through the keyhole, maketh glad;
And through the broken edge of tiles
Into the laddered hayloft smiles.

Meantime, his golden face around
He bares to all the garden ground,
And sheds a warm and glittering look
Among the ivy's inmost nook.

Above the hills, along the blue,
Round the bright air with footing true.
To please the child, to paint the rose,
The gardener of the world, he goes.

Robert Louis Stevenson

NESTING TIME

Wrens and robins in the hedge,
    Wrens and robins here and there;
Building, perching, pecking, fluttering,
    Everywhere!

Christina Rossetti

HURT NO LIVING THING

Hurt no living thing:
    Ladybird, nor butterfly,
Nor moth with dusty wing,
    Nor cricket chirping cheerily,
Nor grasshopper so light of leap,
    Nor dancing gnat, nor beetle fat,
Nor harmless worms that creep.

Christina Rossetti

THE CALL

Come, calf, now to mother,
Come, lamb, that I choose,
Come, cats, one and t'other,
With snowy-white shoes,
Come, gosling all yellow,
Come forth with your fellow,
Come, chickens so small,
Scarce walking at all,
Come, doves, that are mine now,
With feathers so fine now!
The grass is bedewed,
The sunlight renewed,
It's early, early, summer's advancing
But autumn soon comes a-dancing!

Bjornsterne Bjornson

10

BE LIKE THE BIRD

Be like the bird, who
Halting in his flight
On limb too slight
Feels it give way beneath him,
Yet sings,
Knowing he hath wings.

Victor Hugo

IN A CHILD'S ALBUM

Small service is true service while it lasts;
Of humblest friends, bright creature, scorn not one;
The daisy, by the shadow that it casts,
Protects the lingering dewdrop from the sun.

William Wordsworth

KINDNESS TO ANIMALS

Little children, never give
Pain to things that feel and live;
Let the gentle robin come
For the crumbs you save at home;
As his meat you throw along
He'll repay you with a song.
Never hurt the timid hare
Peeping from her green grass lair,
Let her come and sport and play
On the lawn at close of day.
The little lark goes soaring high
To the bright windows of the sky,
Singing as if 'twere always spring,
And fluttering on an untired wing —
Oh! let him sing his happy song,
Nor do these gentle creatures wrong.

WYNKEN, BLYNKEN, AND NOD

Wynken, Blynken, and Nod one night
   Sailed off in a wooden shoe —
Sailed on a river of crystal light,
   Into a sea of dew.
"Where are you going, and what do you wish?"
   The old moon asked the three.
"We have come to fish for the herring fish
   That live in this beautiful sea;
   Nets of silver and gold have we!"
       Said Wynken,
       Blynken,
       And Nod.

The old moon laughed and sang a song,
   As they rocked in the wooden shoe,
And the wind that sped them all night long
   Ruffled the waves of dew.
The little stars were the herring fish
   That lived in that beautiful sea —
"Now cast your nets wherever you wish —
   Never afeared are we";
   So cried the stars to the fishermen three:
       Wynken,
       Blynken,
       And Nod.

All night long their nets they threw
   To the stars in the twinkling foam —
Then down from the skies came the wooden shoe,
   Bringing the fishermen home ;
'Twas all so pretty a sail it seemed
   As if it could not be,
And some folks thought 'twas a dream they'd dreamed
   Of sailing that beautiful sea —
   But I shall name you the fishermen three :
      Wynken,
      Blynken,
      And Nod.

Wynken and Blynken are two little eyes,
   And Nod is a little head,
And the wooden shoe that sailed the skies
   Is a wee one's trundle-bed.
So shut your eyes while mother sings
   Of wonderful sights that be,
And you shall see the beautiful things
   As you rock in the misty sea,
   Where the old shoe rocked the fishermen three :
      Wynken,
      Blynken,
      And Nod.

Eugene Field

THE SUGARPLUM TREE

Have you ever heard of the Sugarplum Tree?
    'Tis a marvel of great renown!
It blooms on the shore of the Lollipop Sea
    In the garden of Shut-eye Town;
The fruit that it bears is so wondrously sweet
    (As those who have tasted it say)
That good little children have only to eat
    Of that fruit to be happy next day.

When you've got to the tree, you would have
        a hard time
    To capture the fruit which I sing;
The tree is so tall that no person could climb
    To the boughs where the sugarplums
        swing!
But up in that tree sits a chocolate cat,
    And a gingerbread dog prowls below —
And this is the way you contrive to get at
    Those sugarplums tempting you so:

You say but the word to that gingerbread dog
    And he barks with such terrible zest
That the chocolate cat is at once all agog,
    As her swelling proportions attest.
And the chocolate cat goes cavorting around
    From this leafy limb unto that,
And the sugarplums tumble, of course, to the
        ground —
    Hurrah for that chocolate cat!

There are marshmallows, gumdrops, and
        peppermint canes,
    With stripings of scarlet or gold,
And you carry away of the treasure that
        rains
    As much as your apron can hold!
So come, little child, cuddle close to me
    In your dainty white nightcap and gown,
And I'll rock you away to that Sugarplum
        Tree
    In the garden of Shut-eye Town.

Eugene Field

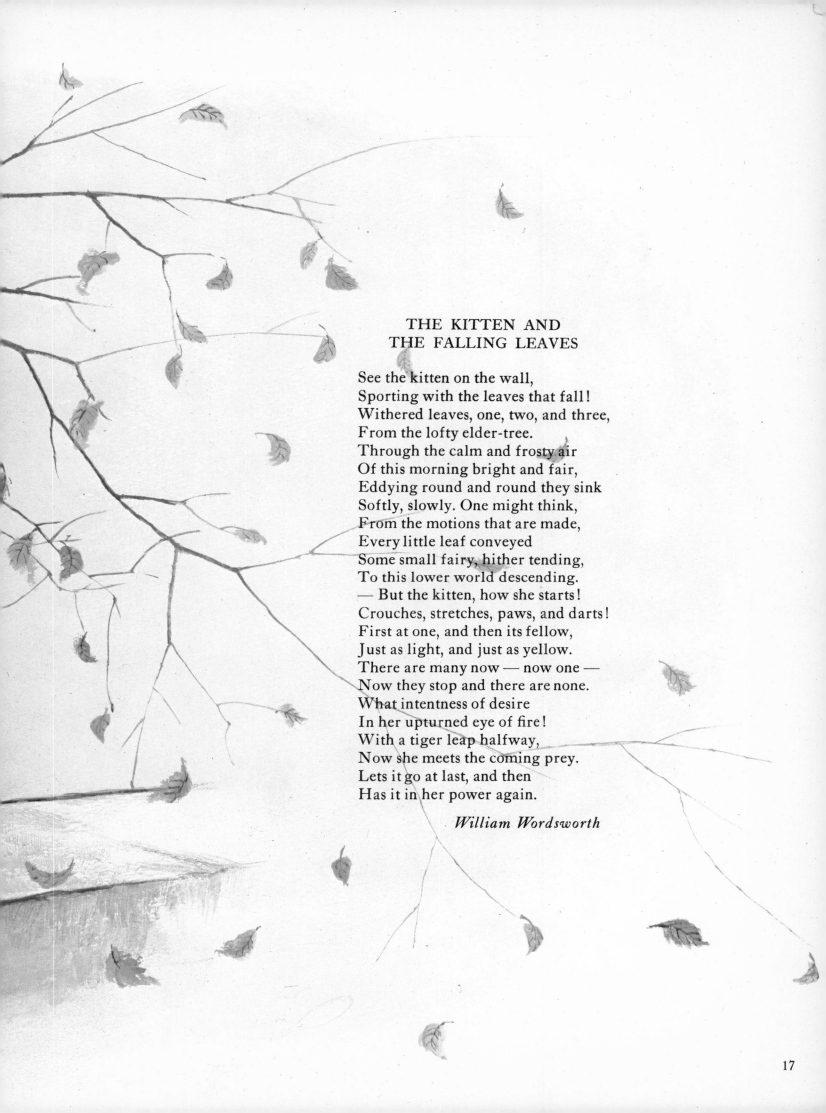

THE KITTEN AND
THE FALLING LEAVES

See the kitten on the wall,
Sporting with the leaves that fall!
Withered leaves, one, two, and three,
From the lofty elder-tree.
Through the calm and frosty air
Of this morning bright and fair,
Eddying round and round they sink
Softly, slowly. One might think,
From the motions that are made,
Every little leaf conveyed
Some small fairy, hither tending,
To this lower world descending.
— But the kitten, how she starts!
Crouches, stretches, paws, and darts!
First at one, and then its fellow,
Just as light, and just as yellow.
There are many now — now one —
Now they stop and there are none.
What intentness of desire
In her upturned eye of fire!
With a tiger leap halfway,
Now she meets the coming prey.
Lets it go at last, and then
Has it in her power again.

William Wordsworth

THE LITTLE ELFMAN

I met a little elfman once,
    Down where the lilies blow.
I asked him why he was so small,
    And why he didn't grow.

He slightly frowned, and with his eye
    He looked me through and through —
"I'm just as big for me," said he,
    "As you are big for you!"

John Kendrick Bangs

THE LILY PRINCESS

Down from her dainty head
The Lily Princess lightly drops
A spider's airy thread.

GOOD MORNING, MERRY SUNSHINE

Good morning, merry sunshine,
How did you wake so soon?
You've scared the little stars away,
And shined away the moon;
I saw you go to sleep last night,
Before I ceased my playing.
How did you get 'way over here,
And where have you been staying?

I never go to sleep, dear;
I just go round to see
My little children of the East
Who rise and watch for me.
I waken all the birds and bees,
And flowers on the way,
And last of all the little child
Who stayed out late to play.

THE CITY MOUSE AND THE GARDEN MOUSE

The city mouse lives in a house;
    The garden mouse lives in a bower,
He's friendly with the frogs and toads,
    And sees the pretty plants in flower.

The city mouse eats bread and cheese;
    The garden mouse eats what he can;
We will not grudge him seeds and stocks,
    Poor little timid furry man.

Christina Rossetti

TREES

The oak is called the king of trees;
The aspen quivers in the breeze;
The poplar grows up straight and tall;
The pear tree spreads along the wall;
The sycamore gives pleasant shade;
The willow droops in watery glade;
The fir tree useful timber gives;
The beech amid the forest lives.

Sara Coleridge

THE MOUNTAIN AND THE SQUIRREL

The mountain and the squirrel
Had a quarrel,
And the former called the latter "Little prig":
Bun replied,
"You are doubtless very big;
But all sorts of things and weather
Must be taken in together
To make up a year,
And a sphere.
And I think it no disgrace
To occupy my place.
If I'm not so large as you,
You are not so small as I,
And not half so spry.
I'll not deny you make
A very pretty squirrel track.
Talents differ; all is well and wisely put,
If I cannot carry forests on my back,
Neither can you crack a nut."

Ralph Waldo Emerson

HOW THEY SLEEP

Some things go to sleep in such a funny way:
Little birds stand on one leg and tuck their heads
    away;

Chickens do the same, standing on their perch;
Little mice lie soft and still, as if they were in
    church;

Kittens curl up close in such a funny ball;
Horses hang their sleepy heads and stand still in
    a stall;

Sometimes dogs stretch out, or curl up in a heap;
Cows lie down upon their sides when they would
    go to sleep.

But little babies dear are snugly tucked in beds,
Warm with blankets, all so soft, and pillows for
    their heads.

Bird and beast and babe — I wonder which of all
Dream the dearest dreams that down from
    dreamland fall!

FOUR DUCKS ON A POND

Four ducks on a pond,
A grass bank beyond,
A blue sky of spring,
White clouds on the wing;
What a little thing
To remember for years —
To remember with tears!

William Allingham

SUSAN BLUE

Oh, Susan Blue,
How do you do?
Please may I go for a walk with you?
Where shall we go?
Oh, I know —
Down in the meadow where the cowslips
    grow!

Kate Greenaway

CERTAINTY

I never saw a moor,
I never saw the sea;
Yet know I how the heather looks,
And what a wave must be.

I never spoke with God,
Nor visited in Heaven;
Yet certain am I of the spot
As if the chart were given.

Emily Dickinson

A CRADLE SONG

Golden slumbers kiss your eyes,
Smiles awake you when you rise.
Sleep, pretty wantons, do not cry,
And I will sing a lullaby:
Rock them, rock them, lullaby.

Care is heavy, therefore, sleep you;
You are care, and care must keep you.
Sleep, pretty wantons, do not cry,
And I will sing a lullaby:
Rock them, rock them, lullaby.

Thomas Dekker

OLD DOG

OLD DOG,
Why do you lie so still?
Are you thinking of when you were a pup?
Are you longing to be a pup?

OLD DOG,
Why do you lie so still?
Do you remember your mother?
Do you want your mother near you?

OLD DOG,
Why do you lie so still?
You must be dreaming of childhood.
You must be afraid to die.

OLD DOG,
Why do you lie so still?
Will you never wake up?
Won't you ever wake up?

Ann Covici

THE MONTHS

January brings the snow,
Makes our feet and fingers glow.

February brings the rain,
Thaws the frozen lake again.

May brings flocks of pretty lambs,
Skipping by their fleecy dams.

June brings tulips, lilies, roses,
Fills the children's hands with posies.

Warm September brings the fruit;
Sportsmen then begin to shoot.

Fresh October brings the pheasant;
Then to gather nuts is pleasant.

March brings breezes loud and shrill,
Stirs the dancing daffodil.

April brings the primrose sweet,
Scatters daisies at our feet.

Hot July brings cooling showers,
Apricots and gillyflowers.

August brings the sheaves of corn;
Then the harvest home is borne.

Dull November brings the blast,
When the leaves are whirling fast.

Chill December brings the sleet,
Blazing fires and Christmas treat.

Sara Coleridge

THE GRASSHOPPER
AND THE ELEPHANT

Way down south where bananas grow,
A grasshopper stepped on an elephant's
  toe.
The elephant said, with tears in his eyes,
"Pick on somebody your own size."

THE OWL AND THE PUSSYCAT

The Owl and the Pussycat went to sea
    In a beautiful pea-green boat;
They took some honey, and plenty of money
    Wrapped up in a five-pound note.
The Owl looked up to the stars above,
    And sang to a small guitar,
"O lovely Pussy, O Pussy, my love,
    What a beautiful Pussy you are,
      You are,
      You are!
    What a beautiful Pussy you are!"

Pussy said to the Owl, "You elegant fowl,
    How charmingly sweet you sing!
Oh! let us be married; too long we have
       tarried:
    But what shall we do for a ring?"
They sailed away, for a year and a day,
    To the land where the bong-tree grows,
And there in a wood a Piggy-wig stood,
    With a ring at the end of his nose,
      His nose,
      His nose,
    With a ring at the end of his nose.

"Dear Pig, are you willing to sell for one
       shilling
    Your ring?" Said the Piggy, "I will."
So they took it away, and were married next
       day
    By the turkey who lives on the hill.
They dined on mince and slices of quince,
    Which they ate with a runcible spoon;
And hand in hand, on the edge of the sand,
    They danced by the light of the moon,
      The moon,
      The moon,
    They danced by the light of the moon.

Edward Lear

SAILING

I see a ship a-sailing, sailing, sailing,
I see a ship a-sailing, sailing out to sea ;
The captain at the railing, railing, railing,
The captain at the railing waves his hand to me.

I see a ship a-rolling, rolling, rolling,
I see a ship a-rolling, rolling home from sea ;
I hear its bell a-tolling, tolling, tolling,
I hear its bell a-tolling, coming back to me.

TO SEE A WORLD

To see a world in a grain of sand
And a heaven in a wild flower,
Hold Infinity in the palm of your hand
And Eternity in an hour.

William Blake

THE ROCK

By a flat rock on the shore of the sea
My dear one spoke to me. Wild thyme
Now grows by the rock
And a sprig of rosemary.

A SEA SONG FROM THE SHORE

Hail! Ho!
Sail! Ho!
Ahoy! Ahoy! Ahoy!
Who calls to me,
So far at sea?
Only a little boy!

Sail! Ho!
Hail! Ho!
The sailor he sails the sea:
I wish he would capture
A little sea horse
And send him home to me.

I wish, as he sails
Through the tropical gales
He would catch me a sea bird, too,
With its silver wings
And the song it sings,
And its breast of down and dew!

I wish he would catch me
A little mermaid,
Some island where he lands,
With her dripping curls,
And her crown of pearls,
And the looking glass in her hands!

Hail! Ho!
Sail! Ho!
Sail far o'er the fabulous main!
And if I were a sailor,
I'd sail with you,
Though I never sailed back again.

James Whitcomb Riley

THE FAIRIES

Up the airy mountain,
    Down the rushy glen,
We daren't go a-hunting,
    For fear of little men.
Wee folk, good folk,
    Trooping all together;
Green jacket, red cap,
    And white owl's feather!

Down along the rocky shore
    Some make their home.
They live on crispy pancakes
    Of yellow tide-foam;
Some in the reeds
    Of the black mountain lake,
With frogs for their watchdogs,
    All night awake.

William Allingham

THE VIOLET

A violet by a mossy stone,
Half hidden from the eye,
Fair as a star, when only one
Is shining in the sky.

William Wordsworth

W

The King sent for his wise men all
   To find a rhyme for W.
When they had thought a good long time
But could not think of a single rhyme,
   "I'm sorry," said he, "to trouble you."

James Reeves

ONE MARCH DAY

As I went walking, one March day,
   Down the length of Blossom Street,
Round me whirled a wind at play,
   And lifted me right off my feet.

English Rhyme

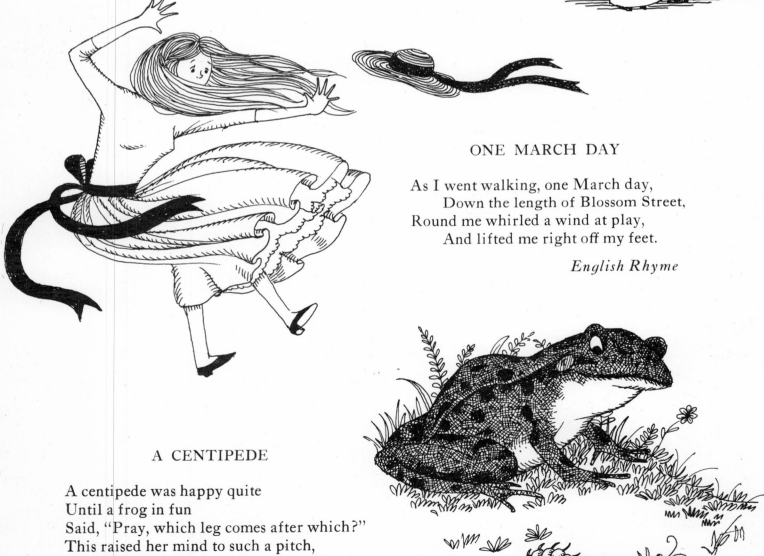

A CENTIPEDE

A centipede was happy quite
Until a frog in fun
Said, "Pray, which leg comes after which?"
This raised her mind to such a pitch,
She lay distracted in a ditch,
Considering how to run.

A KITE

I often sit and wish that I
Could be a kite up in the sky,
And ride upon the breeze and go
Whichever way I chanced to blow.
Then I could look beyond the town,
And see the river winding down,
And follow all the ships that sail
Like me before the merry gale,
Until at last with them I came
To some place with a foreign name.

Frank Dempster Sherman

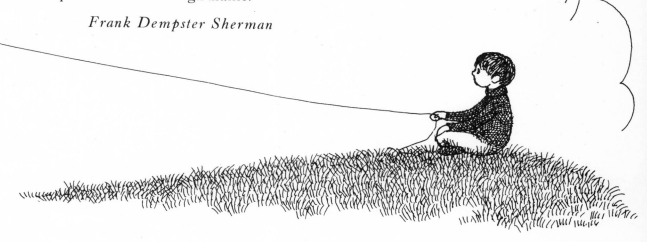

PEDIGREE

The pedigree of honey
Does not concern the bee;
A clover, any time, to him
Is aristocracy.

Emily Dickinson

CARPENTERS

Saw, saw, saw away,
Saw the boards and saw the timbers.
Saw, saw, saw away,
We will build a house today.

MY VALENTINE

I will make you brooches and toys for your delight
Of bird song at morning and starshine at night.
I will make a palace fit for you and me,
Of green days in forests
And blue days at sea.

Robert Louis Stevenson

THE DUEL

The gingham dog and the calico cat
Side by side on the table sat;
'Twas half-past twelve, and (what do you think!)
Nor one nor t' other had slept a wink!
  The old Dutch clock and the Chinese plate
  Appeared to know as sure as fate
There was going to be a terrible spat.
  (I wasn't there; I simply state
  What was told to me by the Chinese plate!)

The gingham dog went, "Bow-wow-wow!"
And the calico cat replied, "Mee-ow!"
The air was littered, an hour or so,
With bits of gingham and calico,
  While the old Dutch clock in the chimney-place
  Up with its hands before its face,
For it always dreaded a family row!
  (Now mind: I'm only telling you
  What the old Dutch clock declares is true!)

The Chinese plate looked very blue,
And wailed, "Oh, dear! what shall we do!"
But the gingham dog and the calico cat
Wallowed this way and tumbled that,
  Employing every tooth and claw
  In the awfullest way you ever saw —
And, oh! how the gingham and calico flew!
  (Don't fancy I exaggerate —
  I got my news from the Chinese plate!)

Next morning, where the two had sat
They found no trace of dog or cat;
And some folks think unto this day
That burglars stole that pair away!
  But the truth about the cat and pup
  Is this: they ate each other up!
Now what do you really think of that!
  (The old Dutch clock it told me so,
  And that is how I came to know.)

                Eugene Field

THE MILK JUG

(The Kitten Speaks)

The Gentle Milk Jug blue and white
    I love with all my soul;
She pours herself with all her might
    To fill my breakfast bowl.

All day she sits upon the shelf,
    She does not jump or climb —
She only waits to pour herself
    When 'tis my suppertime.

And when the Jug is empty quite,
    I shall not mew in vain,
The Friendly Cow all red and white,
    Will fill her up again.

Oliver Herford

CHOOSING A KITTEN

A black-nosed kitten will slumber all the day;
A white-nosed kitten is ever glad to play;
A yellow-nosed kitten will answer to your call;
And a gray-nosed kitten I like best of all.

I HAD A LITTLE DOGGY

I had a little Doggy that used to sit and beg;
But Doggy tumbled down the stairs and broke his little leg.
Oh! Doggy, I will nurse you, and try to make you well,
And you shall have a collar with a little silver bell.

Ah! Doggy, don't you think that you should very faithful be,
For having such a loving friend to comfort you as me?
And when your leg is better, and you can run and play,
We'll have a scamper in the fields and see them making hay.

But, Doggy, you must promise (and mind your word to keep)
Not once to tease the little lambs, or run among the sheep;
And then the little yellow chicks that play upon the grass,
You must not even wag your tail to scare them as you pass.

WHAT DOES LITTLE BIRDIE SAY?

What does little birdie say,
In her nest at peep of day?
"Let me fly," says little birdie,
    "Mother, let me fly away."
"Birdie, rest a little longer,
Till the little wings are stronger."
So she rests a little longer,
    Then she flies away.

What does little baby say,
In her bed at peep of day?
Baby says, like little birdie,
    "Let me rise and fly away."
"Baby, sleep a little longer,
Till the little limbs are stronger."
If she sleeps a little longer,
    Baby, too, shall fly away.

Alfred, Lord Tennyson

THE OAK

Live thy life,
    Young and old,
Like yon oak,
Bright in spring,
    Living gold;

Summer-rich
    Then; and then
Autumn-changed,
Soberer-hued
    Gold again.

All his leaves
    Fallen at length,
Look, he stands,
Trunk and bough,
    Naked strength.

Alfred, Lord Tennyson

HEIGH HO!

Heigh Ho! Time creeps but slow;
    I've looked up the hill so long;
None come this way, the sun sinks low,
    And my shadow's very long.

Kate Greenaway

THE BROOMSTICK TRAIN

Look out! Look out, boys! Clear the track!
The witches are here! They've all come back!
They hanged them high. No use! No use!
What cares a witch for the hangman's noose?
They buried them deep, but they wouldn't lie still,
For cats and witches are hard to kill;
They swore they shouldn't and wouldn't die —
Books said they did, but they lie! they lie!

Oliver Wendell Holmes

THE CLUCKING HEN

"Will you take a walk with me,
    My little wife, today?
There's barley in the barley field,
    And hayseed in the hay."

"Thank you," said the clucking hen.
    "I've something else to do;
I'm busy sitting on my eggs,
    I cannot walk with you."

The clucking hen sat on her nest,
    She made it on the hay;
And warm and snug beneath her breast
    A dozen white eggs lay.

CRACK! CRACK! went all the eggs,
    Out dropped the chickens small.
"Cluck!" said the clucking hen.
    "Now I have you all.

Come along, my little chicks,
    I'll take a walk with you."
"Hello!" said the rooster.
    "Cock-a-doodle-doo!"

ALWAYS FINISH

If a task is once begun,
Never leave it till it's done.
Be the labor great or small,
Do it well or not at all.

39

THE MOON SHIP

In the ocean of the sky,
Borne on rising waves of cloud,
The moon ship
Goes a-gliding by
Through a forest of stars.

From the Japanese.

NIGHT BLESSING

Good night,
Sleep tight,
Wake up bright
In the morning light
To do what's right
With all your might.

SWEET AND LOW

Sweet and low, sweet and low,
    Wind of the western sea!
Low, low, breathe and blow,
    Wind of the western sea!
Over the rolling waters go,
Come from the dying moon, and blow,
    Blow him again to me;
While my little one, while my pretty one
    sleeps.

Sleep and rest, sleep and rest,
    Father will come to thee soon;
Rest, rest, on Mother's breast,
    Father will come to thee soon;
Father will come to his babe in the nest,
Silver sails all out of the west
    Under the silver moon:
Sleep, my little one, sleep, my pretty one,
    sleep.

Alfred, Lord Tennyson

THE ICHTHYOSAURUS

There once was an Ichthyosaurus
Who lived when the earth was all porous,
But he fainted with shame
When he first heard his name,
And departed a long time before us.

CATERPILLAR

Brown and furry
Caterpillar in a hurry
Take your walk
To the shady leaf, or stalk,
Or what not,
Which may be the chosen spot.
No toad spy you,
Hovering bird of prey pass by you;
Spin and die,
To live again a butterfly.

Christina Rossetti

A RULE FOR BIRDS' NESTERS

The robin and the redbreast,
    The robin and the wren;
If ye take out o' their nest,
    Ye'll never thrive agen!

The robin and the redbreast,
    The martin and the swallow;
If ye touch one o' their eggs,
    Bad luck will surely follow!

THE YOUNG LADY OF NIGER

There was a young lady of Niger
Who smiled as she rode on a tiger;
    They returned from the ride
    With the lady inside,
And the smile on the face of the tiger.

A BIRD

A bird came down the walk:
He did not know I saw;
He bit an angleworm in halves
And ate the fellow, raw.

And then he drank a dew
From a convenient grass,
And then hopped sidewise to the wall
To let a beetle pass.

Emily Dickinson

WHO HAS SEEN THE WIND?

Who has seen the wind?
    Neither I nor you;
But when the leaves hang trembling,
    The wind is passing through.

Who has seen the wind?
    Neither you nor I:
But when the trees bow down their heads,
    The wind is passing by.

Christina Rossetti

THE FRIENDLY COW

The friendly cow, all red and white,
    I love with all my heart;
She gives me cream, with all her might,
    To eat with apple tart.

She wanders lowing here and there,
    And yet she cannot stray,
All in the pleasant open air,
    The pleasant light of day.

And blown by all the winds that pass
    And wet with all the showers,
She walks among the meadow grass
    And eats the meadow flowers.

Robert Louis Stevenson

LITTLE WIND

Little wind, blow on the hilltop;
Little wind, blow on the plain,
Little wind, blow up the sunshine,
Little wind, blow off the rain.

THE TWENTY-FOURTH OF DECEMBER

The clock ticks slowly, slowly in the hall,
And slower and more slow the long hours crawl;
It seems as though today
Would never pass away;
The clock ticks slowly, s-l-o-w-l-y in the hall.

SNOWFLAKES

Out of the bosom of the air,
    Out of the cloud-folds of her garments shaken,
Over the woodland brown and bare,
    Over the harvest fields forsaken,
Silent, and soft, and slow
    Descends the snow.

Henry Wadsworth Longfellow

MY GIFT

What can I give Him,
Poor as I am;
If I were a shepherd,
I would give Him a lamb.
If I were a wise man,
I would do my part.
But what can I give Him?
I will give my heart.

Christina Rossetti

AN OLD CHRISTMAS GREETING

Sing hey! Sing hey!
For Christmas Day,
Twine mistletoe and holly,
For friendship glows
In winter snows,
And so let's all be jolly.

Nursery Rhyme

CHRISTMAS HEARTH RHYME

Sing we all merrily,
    Christmas is here,
The day we love best
    Of all days in the year.

Bring forth the holly,
    The box and the bay,
Deck out our cottage
    For glad Christmas day.

Sing we all merrily,
    Draw near the fire,
Sister and brother,
    Grandson and sire.

Old English

CHRISTMAS IN THE OLDEN TIME

Heap on more wood! The wind is chill;
But let it whistle as it will.
We'll keep our Christmas merry still.

Sir Walter Scott

WINTER

Bread and milk for breakfast,
    And woolen frocks to wear,
And a crumb for robin redbreast
    On the cold days of the year.

Christina Rossetti

CHRISTMAS BELLS

I heard the bells on Christmas Day
Their old, familiar carols play,
      And wild and sweet
      The words repeat
Of peace on earth, good will to men!

And thought how, as the day had come,
The belfries of all Christendom
      Had rolled along
      The unbroken song
Of peace on earth, good will to men!

Till, ringing, singing, on its way,
The world revolved from night to day,
      A voice, a chime,
      A chant sublime
Of peace on earth, good will to men!

Henry Wadsworth Longfellow

SANTA CLAUS AND THE MOUSE

One Christmas, when Santa Claus
  Came to a certain house,
To fill the children's stockings there,
  He found a little mouse.

"A Merry Christmas, little friend,"
  Said Santa good and kind.
"The same to you, sir," said the mouse,
  "I thought you wouldn't mind,

If I should stay awake tonight
  And watch you for a while."
"You're very welcome, little mouse,"
  Said Santa, with a smile.

And then he filled the stockings up
  Before the mouse could wink —
From toe to top, from top to toe,
  There wasn't left a chink.

"Now they won't hold another thing,"
  Said Santa Claus with pride.
A twinkle came in mouse's eyes,
  But humbly he replied:

"It's not polite to contradict —
  Your pardon I implore —
But in the fullest stocking there
  I could put one thing more."

"Oh, ho!" laughed Santa. "Silly mouse,
    Don't I know how to pack?
By filling stockings all these years
    I should have learned the knack."

And then he took the stocking down
    From where it hung so high,
And said, "Now put in one thing more,
    I give you leave to try."

The mousie chuckled to himself,
    And then he softly stole
Right to the stocking's crowded toe
    And gnawed a little hole!

"Now, if you please, good Santa Claus,
    I've put in one thing more,
For you will own that little hole
    Was not in there before."

How Santa Claus did laugh and laugh!
    And then he gaily spoke,
"Well, you shall have a Christmas cheese
    For that nice little joke!"

If you don't think this story is true,
    Why, I can show to you
The very stocking with the hole
    The little mouse gnawed through!

Emilie Poulsson

DAFFODILS

I wandered lonely as a cloud
That floats on high o'er vales and hills,
When all at once I saw a crowd —
A host of golden daffodils
Beside the lake, beneath the trees,
Fluttering and dancing in the breeze.

Continuous as the stars that shine
And twinkle on the Milky Way,
They stretched in never-ending line
Along the margin of a bay:
Ten thousand saw I, at a glance,
Tossing their heads in sprightly dance.

The waves beside them danced, but they
Out-did the sparkling waves in glee:
A poet could not but be gay,
In such a jocund company:
I gazed — and gazed — but little thought
What wealth the show to me had brought:

For oft, when on my couch I lie
In vacant or in pensive mood,
They flash upon that inward eye
Which is the bliss of solitude;
And then my heart with pleasure fills,
And dances with the daffodils.

William Wordsworth

THE ELF AND THE DORMOUSE

Under a toadstool crept a wee elf,
Out of the rain, to shelter himself.

Under the toadstool, sound asleep,
Sat a big dormouse all in a heap.

Trembled the wee elf, frightened, and yet
Fearing to fly away lest he get wet.

To the next shelter — maybe a mile!
Sudden the wee elf smiled a wee smile,

Tugged till the toadstool toppled in two,
Holding it over him, gayly he flew.

Soon he was safe home, dry as could be,
Soon woke the dormouse — "Good gracious me!

Where is my toadstool?" loud he lamented.
And that's how umbrellas first were invented.

Oliver Herford

RAIN

The rain is raining all around,
    It falls on field and tree;
It rains on the umbrellas here,
    And on the ships at sea.

Robert Louis Stevenson

APRIL FOOL'S DAY

The first of April, some do say,
Is set apart for All Fools' day,
But why the people call it so
Nor I, nor they themselves, do know.

Old English Almanac

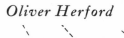

SWEET PEAS

Here are sweet peas, on tiptoe for a flight,
With wings of gentle flush o'er delicate white,
And taper fingers catching at all things,
To bind them all about with tiny rings.

John Keats

"CROAK!" SAID THE TOAD

"Croak!" said the toad. "I'm hungry, I think.
Today I've had nothing to eat or to drink.
I'll crawl to a garden and jump through the pales,
And there I'll dine nicely on slugs and on snails."

"Ho, ho!" quoth the frog. "Is that what you mean?
Then I'll hop away to the next meadow stream.
There I will drink, and eat worms and slugs, too,
And then I shall have a good dinner like you."

Old Garden Rhyme

THE SWAN

Swan swam over the sea —
   Swim, swan, swim;
Swan swam back again,
   Well swam, swan.

GO TO THE ANT

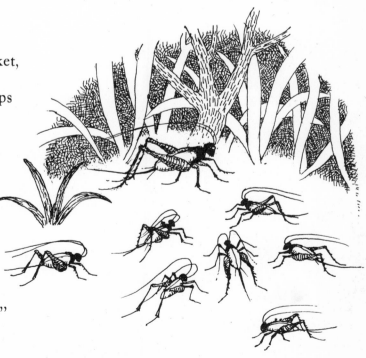

Go to the ant, thou sluggard;
Consider her ways, and be wise:
Which having no guide,
Overseer, or ruler,
Provideth her meat in the summer,
And gathereth her food in the harvest.

The Book of Proverbs

OLD DAME CRICKET

   Old Dame Cricket, down in the thicket,
Brought up her children nine —
   Queer little chaps, in glossy black caps
And brown little suits so fine.

   "My children," she said,
   "The birds are abed:
Go and make the dark earth glad!
   Chirp while you can!"
   And then she began,
Till, oh, what a concert they had!

   They hopped with delight,
   They chirped all night,
Singing, "Cheer up! Cheer up! Cheer!"
   Old Dame Cricket,
   Down in the thicket,
Sat awake till dawn to hear.

A BOY'S SONG

Where the pools are bright and deep,
Where the gray trout lies asleep,
Up the river, and over the lea,
That's the way for Billy and me.

Where the blackbird sings the latest,
Where the hawthorne blooms the sweetest,
Where the nestlings chirp and flee,
That's the way for Billy and me.

Where the mowers mow the cleanest,
Where the hay lies thick and greenest;
There to trace the homeward bee,
That's the way for Billy and me.

Where the hazel bank is steepest,
Where the shadow falls the deepest,
Where the clustering nuts fall free,
That's the way for Billy and me.

James Hogg

COUNTING-OUT RHYMES

Eenie, meenie, minie, mo,
Catch a tiger by the toe,
If he hollers, let him go,
Eenie, meenie, minie, mo.

Out goes the rat,
Out goes the cat,
Out goes the lady
With the big green hat.
Y, O, U, spells you;
O, U, T, spells out!

One potato, two potato,
Three potato, four;
Five potato, six potato,
Seven potato, MORE.

One-ery, Two-ery, Ickery, Ann,
Phillip-son, Phollop-son, Nicholas, John,
Queevy, Quavy,
English Navy,
Zinglum, Zanglum, Bolun, Bun.

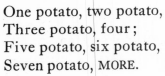

Hinty, minty, cuty, corn,
Apple seed and apple thorn,
Wire, briar, limber lock,
Three geese in a flock.
One flew east, and one flew west,
One flew over the cuckoo's nest.

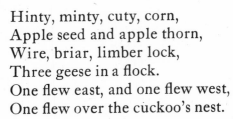

THE BEE

There is a little gentleman
    That wears yellow clothes;
And a dirk below his doublet,
    For sticking of his foes.

He's in a stinging posture
    Wherever him you see,
And if you offer violence,
    He'll stab his dirk in thee.

THE BAREFOOT BOY

Blessings on thee, little man,
Barefoot boy, with cheeks of tan!
With thy turned-up pantaloons,
And thy merry whistled tunes;
With thy red lip, redder still
Kissed by strawberries on the hill;
With the sunshine on thy face,
Through thy torn brim's jaunty grace;
From my heart I give thee joy —
I was once a barefoot boy!

John Greenleaf Whittier

THE MELANCHOLY PIG

There was a pig that sat alone,
    Beside a ruined pump.
By day and night he made his moan:
    It would have stirred a heart of stone
To see him wring his hoofs and groan,
    Because he could not jump.

Lewis Carroll

A YOUNG LADY NAMED BRIGHT

There was a young lady named Bright,
Who traveled much faster than light.
    She started one day
    In the relative way,
And returned on the previous night.

THE KAYAK

Over the briny wave I go,
In spite of the weather, in spite of the snow:
What cares the hardy Eskimo?
In my little skiff, with paddle and lance,
I glide where the foaming billows dance.

Round me the sea-birds slip and soar;
Like me, they love the ocean's roar.
Sometimes a floating iceberg gleams
Above me with its melting streams;
Sometimes a rushing wave will fall
Down on my skiff and cover it all.

But what care I for a wave's attack?
With my paddle I right my little kayak,
And then its weight I speedily trim,
And over the water away I skim.

THE DAY IS DONE

The day is done, and the darkness
  Falls from the wings of Night,
As a feather is wafted downward
  From an eagle in his flight.

I see the lights of the village
  Gleam through the rain and the mist,
And a feeling of sadness comes o'er me
  That my soul cannot resist:

A feeling of sadness and longing,
  That is not akin to pain,
And resembles sorrow only
  As the mist resembles the rain.

Come, read to me some poem,
  Some simple and heartfelt lay,
That shall soothe this restless feeling,
  And banish the thoughts of day.

Not from the grand old masters,
  Not from the bards sublime,
Whose distant footsteps echo
  Through the corridors of Time.

For, like strains of martial music,
  Their mighty thoughts suggest
Life's endless toil and endeavor;
  And tonight I long for rest.

Read from some humbler poet,
  Whose songs gushed from his heart,
As showers from the clouds of summer,
  Or tears from the eyelids start;

Who, through long days of labor,
  And nights devoid of ease,
Still heard in his soul the music
  Of wonderful melodies.

Such songs have power to quiet
  The restless pulse of care,
And come like a benediction
  That follows after prayer.

Then read from the treasured volume
  The poem of thy choice,
And lend to the rhyme of the poet
  The beauty of thy voice.

And the night shall be filled with music,
  And the cares that infest the day,
Shall fold their tents, like the Arabs,
  And as silently steal away.

Henry Wadsworth Longfellow

ANNIE'S GARDEN

In little Annie's garden
  Grew all sorts of posies;
There were pinks, and mignonette,
  And tulips, and roses.

Sweet peas, and morning glories,
  A bed of violets blue,
And marigolds, and asters,
  In Annie's garden grew.

There the bees went for honey,
  And the hummingbirds, too;
And there the pretty butterflies
  And the ladybirds flew.

And there among her flowers,
  Every bright and pleasant day,
In her own pretty garden
  Little Annie went to play.

Eliza Lee Follen

IRIS

Ere yet the sun is high,
All blue the iris blossoms wave,
  The color of the sky.

From the Japanese.

THE SNAIL'S DREAM

A snail who had a way, it seems,
Of dreaming very curious dreams,
Once dream't he was — you'll never guess! —
The Lightning Limited Express.

Oliver Herford